Women and girls face many unique challenges in society,
only some of which are addressed in this book. They are as follows:

1. Understanding female potential
2. Positive body image
3. The importance of girls supporting each other
4. Women in the workplace
5. The gender pay gap
6. Family planning
7. The prevelance of women in history
8. The importance of consent
9. The importance of family leave with a newborn
10. Feminism is for everyone - not just girls
11. Domestic violence & division of domestic labor
12. Women in politics
13. Girls in STEM
14. The "glass ceiling"
15. Public breastfeeding
16. Bullying / cat-calling
17. The importance of female leaders as role models

"Women's status in society has become the standard by which
humanity's progress toward civility and peace can be measured."

–Mahnaz Afkhami

Note to Caregivers:

The poems in this book are meant to spread awareness and encourage discussions with children about gender equality. Gender equality is the fifth of *17 United Nations Sustainable Development Goals* or "Global Goals".

Some of the concepts in the book can be challenging to address with young ones. The topics can be nuanced with subtle layers. As a caregiver, use your best judgement to determine what level of detail is appropriate when explaining the poems.

Whether you are reading this with a little girl or a little boy, *thank you*. Raising feminists is an act of social justice, and has the potential to change the world. A woman empowered can lift generations.

Enjoy! Holly Olsen

Feminist Nursery Rhymes

Alternative poems for gender equality.

For little girls and boys everywhere

Special thanks to my sisters, mother, and all the women in my life!

Written by Holly Olsen

Illustrated by Elie Galih

HER POTENTIAL

She'll be comin' around the mountain when she comes.
She'll be makin' noise of triumph, bangin' drums!
She is brilliant, she's a reader.
She's persistent, tough, a leader.
She'll create and cure and grow as she becomes!

To the tune of:
She'll Be Comin' 'Round the Mountain

Head, shoulders, knees, and toes,
Bodies grow uniquely, so,
Spread your arms,
and hug yours close!
Love your body, head to toe!

To the tune of:
Head, Shoulders, Knees, and Toes

3

There was a girl who had a goal
To always help another:
U-N-I-T-Y! U-N-I-T-Y! U-N-I-T-Y!
For girls* must help each other!

When we unite, we are made strong
Because we work together!
U-N-I-T-Y! U-N-I-T-Y! U-N-I-T-Y!
Let's help all girls* forever!

*and boys!

To the tune of:
BINGO

WOMEN IN THE WORKPLACE

Little Jan Horner
Won't sit in the corner
Watching as jobs go by.
She stands up to run,
And gets the job done.
And says
"What a smart girl am I!"

To the tune of:
Little Jack Horner

EQUAL PAY for EQUAL WORK

Sing a song of recompense:
She worked hard with a guy,
They paid her seven, gave him ten,
And both thought of it, "Why?"

When the office opened,
The two began to say,
"Isn't that an awful trick
To play on girls today?"

To the tune of:

Sing A Song of Sixpense

FAMILY PLANNING

Mary, Mary, sweet canary,
When does her family grow?
Please let her choose and don't accuse.
Her body.
Her choice.
Don't you know?

To the tune of:
Mary, Mary, Quite Contrary

WOMEN IN HISTORY

My friend Dolly has a dream,
E-I-E-I-O!
Where girls abound in history,
E-I-E-I-O!
With a story here, and a photo there,
Here a book, there a song,
Everywhere a girl, strong!
My friend Dolly had a dream.
Help her make it so!

To the tune of:

Old MacDonald Had a Farm

CONSENT

Georgie Porgie, please comply:
To kiss a girl, first ask, "May I?"
Consent is what you need, my friend.
A rule to live by, 'til the end.

To the tune of:

Georgie Porgie

FAMILY LEAVE

Behold Mother Hubbard,
She often had suffered
With newborns and no family leave.
Babies and mothers
Need time to recover;
To bond.
Have respect for them, please.

To the tune of:
Old Mother Hubbard

Polly get your movement on!
Feminism's going strong.
Polly spread the word along
For you and me!

Girls and boys will make it so.
Work together, you will grow,
You can make a difference for
Equality!

To the tune of:
Polly Put the Kettle On

"Equality"

DOMESTIC VIOLENCE &
DIVISION OF DOMESTIC LABOR

Peter, Peter, pumpkin eater,
You've a wife and want to keep her,
Give respect and treat her well,
And that way you can both excel!

Peter, Peter, pumpkin eater,
Share the workload, don't be meager,
Work and help with all the chores.
Yes, do your part, and don't keep score!

To the tune of:
Peter, Peter, Pumpkin Eater

WOMEN IN POLITICS

You put your right hand in,
Then shake some hands about.
You put your best foot forth,
And you try your best, no doubt!

You learn about the issues,
And participate in town.
That's what it's all about!

To the tune of:
The Hokey Pokey

23

13

The little missy shy girl
Thought S.T.E.M. was meant for boys.
That would be so sad
'Cause it's something girls enjoy!
Science, Tech, and Math
And Engineering too,
They are all great subjects
That girls and boys can do!

To the tune of:
The Itsy Bitsy Spider

GLASS CEILING

Lavender's me, dilly, dilly,
Lavender's you.
Hit the ceiling? Dilly, dilly,
You can break through!
It is just glass, dilly, dilly,
You can get past.
You shall climb high, dilly, dilly,
Up to the sky!

To the tune of:
Lavender's Blue

15

Hush little baby, don't say a word,
Mama's gonna feed you as you prefer.
And if some folks scorn what they see,
She'll continue peacefully.
Feeding your baby is always right,
Both in and out, yes, day or night.
Hush little baby, don't you frown.
Mama can feed you all around!

To the tune of:
Hush Little Baby, Don't You Cry

BULLYING / CAT-CALLING

Rub-a-dub-dub
Three girls in a club
And what do you think they hear?
The boys disrespecting,
All fairness neglecting.
Please stop the harassment, my dears!

To the tune of:
Rub-a-dub-dub, Three Men in a Tub

FEMALE LEADERS

Bold Queen Cole was a merry old soul,

And a merry old soul was she!

She called for peace,

And she called for spoons

To feed anyone hungry.

Everybody loved the queen,

For she was always keen.

Oh there's none so rare, as can compare,

With Queen Cole and her ways of peace.

To the tune of:
Old King Cole

"A feminist is anyone who recognizes the equality and full humanity of women and men." —*Gloria Steinem*

"We cannot all succeed when half of us are held back." —*Malala Yousafzai*

"I am not free while any woman is unfree, even when her shackles are very different from my own." —*Audre Lorde*

"Feminism isn't about making women stronger. Women are already strong. It's about changing the way the world perceives that strength." —*G.D Anderson*

"To all the little girls [...], never doubt that you are valuable and powerful and deserving of every chance and opportunity in the world to pursue and achieve your own dreams." —*Hillary Clinton*

"Women belong in all places where decisions are being made... It shouldn't be that women are the exception." —*Ruth Bader Ginsburg*

"Here's to strong women. May we know them. May we be them. May we raise them." —*Unknown*

If you like this book, you are sure to love
Nursery Rhymes for Social Good

It will help teach your children about social justice and the United Nations 17 Sustainable Development Goals (the "Global Goals"). Find it on Amazon.com or visit www.socialgoodbooks.com.

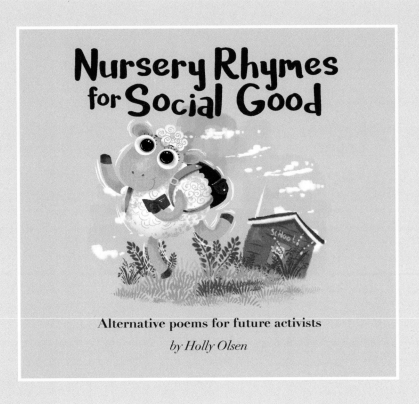

Nursery Rhymes for Social Good

Alternative poems for future activists

by Holly Olsen

ABOUT THE AUTHOR

Holly Olsen is an author and educator. She is the author of *Nursery Rhymes for Social Good*. She co-founded a bilingual preschool with a focus on social and environmental justice. In recent years, she co-founded the nonprofit HemoHelper where she helps provide medical IDs and supplies to hemophiliacs in developing countries. She has a masters degree in Second Language Teaching from Utah State University, and a B.A. in Spanish with a minor in International Studies.